The Simple Profit Multiplier

How To Double, Triple And Quadruple Your Business Profits… While Working Less!

Ian B McConnell - ProfitMarketing101.com

The Simple Profit Multiplier
How To Double, Triple And Quadruple Your Business Profits… While Working Less!

ISBN: 978-1-731-42599-7

Copyright © 2018 Ian B McConnell All rights reserved

ProfitMarketing101.com
P.O. Box A459
Australind, WA 6233
Australia

www.ProfitMarketing101.com

Notice of rights

All rights reserved. No part of this book may be reproduced or transmitted in any form or by any means, electronic, mechanical, photocopying, recording, or otherwise, without the prior written permission of the author.

Disclaimer

This book is presented for informational purposes only. The content is of the nature of general comment, and neither purports, nor intends to give any accounting, legal or other advice. No guarantees or claims are made or implied. Readers should not act on the basis of any matter in this book without first considering, and if appropriate taking, professional advice with due regard to their own particular circumstances. All the content represents the views of the author at the time of publication and is as accurate as is possible to ascertain. The author and publisher will not accept any responsibility for any errors or omissions.

Table of Contents

Notice of Rights	3
Disclaimer	4
Table of Contents	5
How To Get The Best From This Book	7
Introduction	9
Where Are You Now?	11
What Are You Worth?	13
Where Is Your Time Going?	17
How To Improve Your Earnings	21
Why Your Business Is Really A Marketing Business	26
How To Become A Marketing Genius	29
How To Calculate The Lifetime Value Of Your Client	32
The Magic Profit Producing Formula	38
18 Ways To Generate Inquiries	44
15 Ways To Increase Your Conversion From Inquiry To Sale	58
7 Ways To Increase The Number Of Transactions	74
12 Ways To Increase The Transaction Size	79
Know Your Costs, Know Your Profit	87
Now Take Massive Action	91
Final Words	96
My Story	98

Table of Contents (continued)

Appendix	100
Earnings per hour form	101
Earnings per hour example	102
Daily time form	103
Daily time form example	104
Client lifetime value form	105
Client lifetime value example	106
Magic profit producing formula form	107
Magic profit producing formula example	108
Advertising return on investment form	109
Advertising return on investment example	110
Profit and loss form	111
Profit and loss example	112
FAQ example	113
Risk reversal guarantee example	115
Sales letter example	116
Thank You	118

How To Get The Best From This Book

This book should be one of those books that takes a prominent position on your desk every day - it will end up being well worn, dog-eared and full of highlighted points in no time.

It is an information guide that can be used over and over again, no matter what stage of business life you are in and no matter what type of business you are in.

I suggest keeping this book close by. The first time you read it, don't highlight anything – do the highlighting on the 2nd or 3rd pass.

This book should be read and referred to many times. Some tips may apply now while others don't, but in 6 months those that didn't apply may apply then.

It is great learning about this stuff but it will never translate into dollars in your pocket until you **implement the ideas.**

Please have an open mind and try different things. Often Business Owners make the mistake of following everyone else in the industry because that is the way it's always been done.

Dare to be different,
Try something new…
You will be amazed at the result!

Introduction

The idea behind this book is to save you from the costly learning curve of business – it will save you time and money.

It enables you to run rings around your competition as they try and figure out why you are successful and dominating the marketplace.

This book virtually guarantees your business success and multiplied profits if you do the work required. Business is a game – it should be simple and fun. But Business Owners tend to complicate things and the business ends up controlling them.

Owning a business should mean a better lifestyle - flexible and shorter working hours and more money. But this is hardly ever the case; it's more like working 60+ hours a week for about $4 an hour.

Why is this so?

Because Business Owners overlook the basic fundamentals of a business and don't allow it to flourish. They also neglect to improve themselves.

This book is about those fundamentals, those core principles. You will be amazed at the simplicity with which you will be able to apply these principles and potentially add thousands, tens of thousands and in some cases millions of dollars to your profits.

It doesn't matter whether you sell a service or a product, these principles, when applied, will have a dramatic effect on your bottom line. It will change the way you view, manage, conduct and promote your business forever...

I refer to customers as clients. A customer to me is a one-off purchaser while clients are recurring purchasers who trust and respect your advice and service. They come to your business for an experience not just to buy something.

Where Are You Now?

If you think you are beaten, you are,
If you think you dare not, you don't.
If you like to win, but you think you can't,
It is almost certain you won't.

If you think you'll lose, you're lost.
For out in the world we will find,
Success begins with a person's will –
It's all in the state of mind.

If you think you are outclassed, you are,
You've got to think high to rise,
You've got to be sure of yourself before
You can ever win a prize.

Life's battles don't always go
To the stronger or faster person,
But sooner or later the person who wins
Is the person who thinks they can!!!

Author Unknown

Business Owners have to play to win. If you don't play to win you will lose and your family will go without more than they should. In the world of owning your own business only YOU can make changes that positively affect your business. Only YOU are to blame if it doesn't work, you can't blame the world.

Where you are now is a direct result of choices you have made in your life until today. If you want to create amazing results you have to take responsibility, take ownership of your business.

Life is full of mistakes… And for you to be successful you have to make those mistakes. You have to play 100%, you have to try different ideas, you have to get creative and you have to persist just like a child trying to walk.

Life is full of obstacles but you only fail when you give up!

What Are You Worth?

We all know a new business needs to save every dollar possible, keep overheads low and maximize the margins…

So the baker bakes his own bread, the hairdresser cuts her clients hair, the shop owner runs their own shop… This is great because you've left a job to chase the self-employed dream… being able to do things your way, double your hourly rate and have flexible working hours.

But often things like downtime and opportunity cost are not considered.

Tasks like administration work, marketing, dealing with suppliers, supplying free quotes, etc can often eat up half of the hours you work per week.

Remember being in business is about working less and having more money.

Take some time to do this exercise –

Take your desired yearly income, divide it by 48 weeks (4 weeks vacation) then by 40 hours. This will give you your desired earning per hour.

Example – If you want to earn $100,000 per year,
divided by 48 weeks = $2,083 per week,
divided by 40 hours = $52 per hour.

You might want to work more or fewer weeks per year and more or fewer hours per week. Adjust them to suit your ideal requirements.

Write it down here:
My desired earning per hour is $_____

Now you have an idea of what your time is worth. This is the amount per hour you have to be earning every working hour or you are not going to meet your yearly income goal. Now some hours you will earn more while some hours you will earn less but the average has to be at least the number you have calculated.

Keep this hourly rate in the back of your mind when you are talking to a sales rep or a time-wasting client… Your time is valuable.

Another eye-opening exercise –

In the Appendix, you will find a "Daily Time Form." Create your own, print 7 copies and each day, for the next 7 consecutive days, record how your time is spent in the business. An example is provided in the Appendix.

At the end of the 7 days, total the hours worked in your business and the profit generated in that week. The profit should be the total sales less the costs associated with those sales.

Associated costs are not only the costs of the product you may be reselling but also the overhead portion - like the rent, car payment, electricity, loan interest. An easy way to calculate the overhead cost for the week is to add them up over a year and divide them by 52 to get a weekly overhead cost.

Be honest, only you will ever see the results.

Divide the weekly profit by the hours worked.

Write it down here:
Actual gross earning per hour is $_____

Actual earning per hour less desired hourly income is $_____

Test and measure task –

In the appendix, you will find an "Earnings per Hour" form. Create your own, print it out and fill in the details of today's findings. On a weekly basis you need to fill in that week's results. Your goal is to constantly increase your actual earnings per week.

Keep all your forms in one file as you will refer to them often. Call it your "Business Growth File." This file will provide the clarity in your business life and help you to succeed.

The difference between your actual earning per hour and your desired earning per hour may surprise you, but it gives you a starting point.

In 9 out of 10 cases, Business Owners realize their actual earnings per hour are much lower than when they had a JOB (**J**ust **O**ver **B**roke.)

But don't despair you are like 90% of other Business Owners. Read on to find out how to correct this very quickly.

Where Is Your Time Going?

I smile when I talk to Business Owners and they say to me "I don't have time to do that" or "the days are too short." In my first business I suffered from this problem as well, and the truth is you can't afford not to make the time to implement the strategies we teach.

In my first business, I struggled to get everything done. I completed time management courses, I had a daily diary and to-do lists all neatly planned out and prioritized…

But none of it worked for me.

I had all these tasks to do every day, working in and on the business. I just ended up with lists of stuff that never got done. I found I started procrastinating more and more.

I was going backward, things were getting worse.

Every morning I was carrying over 80% of the tasks that I didn't do yesterday. When I got to the end of the week I was totally overwhelmed and depressed because I felt like I wasn't achieving.

Then a business coach showed me the way. He got me to record everything I was doing for a week in a diary. So as I started a task I would record it in my diary. As I finished that task and started a new one I would record it.

At the end of the week, I totaled how much time I had spent on the various tasks. Then I graded the tasks into 4 groups - income-producing activities, marketing, administration and waste of time activities.

To my astonishment, I found that I was spending only 6% of my time on marketing and only 21% on income-producing activities. The balance, a huge 73% of my time was wasted on activities that I could employ someone on a part-time basis for about $12 per hour to complete. My desired hourly rate at that time was $58.

If I continued this way my business would never have grown to the extent that it did and I certainly wouldn't have achieved the sale price I did achieve.

I believed I had to do it all myself to save money… But it was actually costing me much more in the end.

The opportunity cost was high - I was completing the mundane, repetitive administration tasks (that I didn't enjoy doing, so it was taking longer than it should have) and I was neglecting important tasks such as marketing and implementing new strategies.

I was completing a $13 per hour task when I could have been implementing strategies that would have generated $100 per hour or more and brought in hundreds of clients into my sales loop.

As a Business Owner, you have to be certain that every activity you undertake is maximizing the return on investment of your time. Always work with the long-term in mind, not just the short-term rewards.

Time is precious,
we can make more money,
but we can't make more time!

Test and measure task –

Previously we had you complete a daily time form for 7 days to calculate how much time you actually spent in the business.

Now on the same forms highlight tasks that fall into these 4 categories:

1. Income-producing activities,
2. Marketing,
3. Administration and
4. Waste of time activities.

Total the amount of time spent on each category in the week. Then calculate each as a percentage of the total.

For example, if the total hours spent in your business was 60 hours and 12 hours was spent on administration work then 20% of your total business time is used up on administration.

12 divided by 60 = 0.2 x 100 = 20%

How To Improve Your Earnings?

Now you have a good idea where you are spending your time in your business and now it's time to rethink your priorities.

You know where the money is being made in your business and you know that marketing will grow your business. What tasks can you delegate, outsource or automate so that you can spend more time on tasks that will improve your earnings and have a greater long-term benefit?

It is a leap of faith. I remember learning this information in my first business. My excuse was *"but I'm doing this admin stuff after hours, it's not affecting how many hours I'm billing during the day?"*

The truth of the matter is, I could have paid someone $10 an hour to do the administration work on a part-time basis and spent the time after hours learning and applying different marketing strategies or, better still, enjoyed the time with my family.

It is false economy and a mistake to try and do it all. I know you will be thinking *"but now I have to find the extra cash to pay that staff member or the outsourced person or the automation software…"*

Just do it, after you have analyzed the return on investment!

It may be tough the first month, but then the strategies start working… And it just gets better and better. The amount you are paying out in cash or time to implement the changes will be nothing compared to the benefits that will result from this.

It is natural for Business Owners to be "control freaks" because you have dedicated so much effort, time and commitment to your business… it's your baby, it is often very hard to let go.

Being a "control freak" is like trying to drive your car down the road with the brake on. You may move forward slowly but nowhere near as fast as you could go.

But a word of caution, you should never ever hire a person before you have completely exhausted every other avenue first. Look at technology first. Technology today makes it very easy to automate certain tasks. But if automation won't help, look at outsourcing.

Just about everything can be outsourced, and the outsourced person doesn't have to live in the same town or the same country! The internet has made it very easy to outsource tasks that can be emailed or sent over the internet.

If you can't automate or outsource, the very last resort should be to hire someone. But always remember it is going to add substantially to your expenses. You need to carefully consider the return on investment of that hire.

FOCUS, FOCUS, FOCUS on the tasks that bring in the money and grow the business.
Don't get bogged down with stuff that doesn't!

Calculating where your time is going normally surprises people because they realize that they are actually spending a small percentage of their time on income-producing tasks and almost no time on marketing.

The non income-producing activities tend to clutter and distract Business Owners.

Leverage is the name of the game. Getting more out of less. Find ways that you can earn income without having to physically complete the work yourself. This is a solution that will bring success, more money and more time without any extra work.

If you were a "Marketing Genius" and you could put promotions and systems in place that would:

- Provide a constant stream of new clients that converted well.
- Your existing clients continued to come back and purchase on a regular basis.
- And, you were able to double your profit margin.

Would you continue to do the work yourself?

Imagine the leverage by having 4 or 5 people doing what you used to do and you make a profit from each one of them.

At this stage you may be struggling to find enough work for yourself, some months you are worked off your feet, then the next you are standing around looking for work. This is very common in businesses and in 9 out of 10 cases it is due to the Business Owner not knowing how to market effectively.

If you learn how to market effectively you are in complete control… You decide how much business you want… You decide if you want to grow the business from you being constantly busy to having 1 or 3 or 10 employees/ subcontractors / outsourced services.

Marketing is an essential skill in business. It provides the keys to the vehicle that will take you anywhere you want to go as fast or as slow as you like!

But Marketing should never be delegated or outsourced because it is an incredibly important factor of your success!

Why Your Business Is Really A Marketing Business.

Cash flow comes from income-producing tasks and future sales and growth come from the marketing. If you are spending the minority of your time on these tasks you will not survive!

Sorry to be so blunt, but it is the honest truth. If you spend time on the wrong activities, you will not only work much harder than you need to, but every day you will take 2 steps forward and 3 back!

Businesses start and fail at an alarming rate. Statistics tell us that in the US over a million people start a business of some type. Within 12 months of starting 40% will have failed. Within 5 years 80% would have failed. And if you've survived 5 years don't relax because 80% of businesses that survive the first 5 years fail within the next 5 years.

Why? With all the information available why do such a high percentage of businesses fail?

Because Business Owners focus on the wrong activities!

Think back to when you had a JOB (Just Over Broke) and you where the person doing the work. Your focus was to be good at whatever work you did. Now you're a Business Owner and your business does the work.

But your clients have choices. They can choose between you or your competitor. Both businesses offer the same perceived service or product to that client – even though you may not think so.

A fatal assumption is to think that if you do your job well the clients will come.

It's fatal because while word of mouth may happen to a small extent initially, it will certainly not be enough to create the lifestyle you require. Truthfully, it won't even be enough to survive.

The business that is a great marketer of its services and product will always win. They may not have the best product or service but their marketing will always help them to succeed.

Take a moment to think of great businesses in your local area and I guarantee that they are very proactive with their marketing. You'll find the large businesses are pushing their branding while the smaller business will be using effective and low-cost direct marketing techniques.

You need to become an effective marketer of whatever product or service you sell. You need to become a "Marketing Genius."

How To Become A Marketing Genius

I hope by now I have convinced you that to be successful in business it is imperative that you become a Marketer of whatever service or product you sell.

However, you will need to get rid of any marketing approach you have had in the past… You need to be open to new ideas… You need to realize that marketing is not an expense.

The majority of businesses that I have come across focus on cost reduction. They focus their energy on reducing costs so they end up doing the administration work; they end up doing the packing, the sorting. They end up working long hours just to save costs and end up by adding 10 or 20% to their profits.

If they took this same energy and focused it on marketing the addition to the profits is limitless.

At least 50% of your time should be dedicated to marketing and the other 50% to the operation of the business.

Anyone can create a business that is just another JOB (Just Over Broke) but a great business is one with great cash flow.

Accountants may tell you that Marketing is an expense and when times get tough the advice is usually to cut back on the advertising.

But the truth is marketing can be your best investment when done properly. If you run an advertisement that costs $300 and it generates $1,800 of profit in 30 days, I would say that was an excellent investment. The best thing is once you know the advertisement works you are able to use it over and over again for many years.

Marketing is only an expense when done incorrectly.

Testing and measuring constantly is a critical component of being a marketing genius. You cannot manage what you can't measure. Every time someone walks through your door, calls your business or enquires through any means ask them this simple question "How did you hear about us" and keep a tally.

This tally will tell you what advertising is working and you can then make decisions. Advertising that doesn't bring results within a week should be adjusted or canceled. Advertising with mediocre results can be massaged to try and improve the results, while the advertising that is working you leave well alone.

There is no sense in spending $150 on advertising that produces sales of $50. This is when an Accountant may say "I told you so, marketing is an expense!"

Marketing should be like a tap, when it's opened profits pour out. You should have your hand firmly on that tap regulating the amount of profits that pour out.

How To Calculate The Lifetime Value Of Your Client?

The lifetime value of your client is the total profit generated over the lifetime of his or her patronage to your business.

Say an average client generates an average profit of $75 on the first sale, then repurchases on average 3 times in 12 months with an average repurchase profit of $150. And the average patronage lifespan is 2 years, then your average lifetime client value is $975.

You could theoretically afford to spend up to $975 to bring in a new client and break even. And that's not including the referrals they may provide in those 2 years.

Business is about creating relationships with people. Most businesses make the fatal mistake of making it far too hard for clients to start a relationship with them. They make it too hard to get potential clients to start trusting them and start using their products or services.

If you take away those hurdles and objections to use your product or service far more people will develop a relationship with you.

If you provide great value, service and results these clients will continue to deal with you. They would have no reason to go anywhere else. The fact that you had faith in your product or service and absorbed the perceived risk will be remembered by the client resulting in loyalty and a client that will talk about your great service.

It is therefore very important to develop those relationships very quickly and nurture them so these clients turn into lifelong clients.

A few years ago I decided I needed to join a gym as I was packing on the weight. The gym had a few deals starting from paying $6 per visit, $49.95 per month for a 6-month membership or $29.95 per month for a 12-month membership.

I knew I needed to visit the gym at least 3 times a week for it to have any benefit. So the 6-month membership would be much cheaper than the $6 per visit… but then the 12-month deal was more attractive again.

So I signed up for the 12-month membership.

My cost per gym visit was about $2.30. The monthly amount is automatically deducted every month out of my bank account and every month I get a free assessment and program update… which is worth more than the monthly fee I believe.

Provided the service remains at the same standard or better I'll probably be visiting that gym until we move out of the area which won't be for many years.

Do you think the gym loses money every month by offering membership gym visits for $2.30 when they could be getting $6? Or do you think they have calculated that if they can get people into the membership those people are likely to keep paying for years to come? I know people (and you probably do too) who have joined, gone religiously for 2 months and stopped going, but continued paying their monthly membership??

By doing this the gym can accurately forecast its cash flow. They know they will receive thousands of dollars next month… even if every single member didn't visit the gym at all that month.

Most businesses fear that the client will come in once and never again so they try and maximize their profits on the first sale.

THE SIMPLE PROFIT MULTIPLIER

This is a fatal mistake because it is 6 times more expensive to sell to a new client than to an existing client. Your existing client has experienced your service, trusts you and has been through your system. If they are happy they will even recommend you!

Many businesses increase their profits and client base by shifting their focus from making a profit on the first sale to making an ongoing profit from repeat purchases over the life of the client.

Now you may have a business that in the past has only dealt with clients once or maybe twice. Like a builder that builds a house for a client, that client won't be building a house every month? That's true but some time later in their life they may build again or they may know someone that wants to build a house.

It is in the builder's best interest to ensure that the client will automatically choose his business the next time they build and without hesitation, the client would recommend the builder to their circle of influence.

A true business is one that acquires a client and sells them something over and over again, even if it means selling them someone else's services or product and you receive a commission.

Like the builder building a house and then offering ongoing maintenance and repair services from strategic alliances that pay him an ongoing commission - a yearly paint touch up service from the painting contractor, a monthly lawn mowing service from the local lawn contractor, a monthly window cleaning service etc.

The commissions may be small but they all add up and it's money that just keeps coming in… The best part is the builder retains contact with the client and puts himself in a terrific position should they, or someone they know, want to build in the future.

I heard of a Refrigeration Mechanic that installs heating and cooling systems in houses and offices. Now once someone has bought a heating and cooling system there is usually no need to buy another one for many years to come, unless they move.

But what he does is sends out a 6 monthly mail out offering a $19.95 service to the unit, which is usually a $49.95 charge. He offers it to his existing clients and also advertises to the market.

Now every service he completes he is actually losing $30 but by testing and measuring, his results show that 49% of people responding to the $19.95 service requested him to complete additional work resulting in an average of $124.00 of profit.

Even though he loses $30 on the initial service, in 49% of cases he makes an average of $124.00 profit. The net result is a great profit and new clients in his system.

Eye-Opening Exercise –

You need to calculate your client's lifetime value. In the Appendix, is a "Client Lifetime Value" form and an example. Create your own, print it out, complete it and file it in your "Business Growth File."

Once you know your client's lifetime value you will not hesitate to spend money to get them into your sales system. If you are paying $100 for a client with a lifetime value of $975 that is a huge 875% return on investment. At that return, you should be buying clients as quickly as you possibly can!

The Magic Profit Producing Formula

After owning many businesses, helping Business Owners, using the services of businesses and networking with Business Owners it is often fascinating how many just don't get it… They just don't understand.

The mechanic that services our cars is a brilliant Mechanic, trustworthy, honest and a great mechanic. His workshop is immaculate, employees are great to talk to and his wife does most of the administration. I go there because he does a great job and charges fairly. I never feel like I've been taken for a ride and am confident that the job is always done right.

He advertises in the local newspaper and that's where his advertising ends. I have never been reminded to bring our cars in for a checkup and I know nothing about the workings of his business. It is a distant relationship – bring in your car when you need to.

Judging by what I can see I would say that his overheads must be fairly high – building mortgage, car repayments, staff wages etc.

I've mentioned in passing that he needs to encourage his clients to come in more frequently, he needs to encourage new clients, he needs to test different headlines in his advertising...

He knows what he should be doing. I can see simple ways that will triple his profit within 60 days... But he is too busy. He is too busy working on cars, getting them repaired, get them out to bring the next one in and it scares me. I am scared for him because he is not building his business, he is not building loyalty, and he is not offering other add-on services like car washing/ detailing, a small dent repair service... anything that could easily be outsourced.

If a competitor opens next door tomorrow and marketed even slightly better he could potentially lose every client he thought he had. The truth is I am not being encouraged to ever return to use his services... I don't feel appreciated.

He is working his backside off but really only has a job. He makes the typical mistake of throwing a few ads in the paper with a few telephone directory listings and then hopes people call or walk in to make it worthwhile.

He can continue this way and he will make some money here and there. But he will always hope that enough people book in their cars next month to cover the overheads and generate some profit…

Or he could follow the "Magic Profit Producing Formula" and build a strong long lasting business.

I'll explain…

Inquiries x Conversion Rate = **No. of Clients**

No. of Clients x Average Transactions per year x Average Profit per Transaction = **Profit per year**

Profit = Sale price less costs associated with that sale.

Now let's try the formula with some numbers and I'll show you how a small 10% increase can magically result in a huge 46% increase in profit.

THE SIMPLE PROFIT MULTIPLIER

	Last year	Add 10%	
Inquiries (the total number of potential clients that call or walk in to your business)	2500	2750	
X	X	X	
Conversion Rate (the percentage of potential clients that you convince to buy)	22%	24.2%	
=	=	=	
No. of Clients (they have bought)	550	665	21% increase
X	X	X	
Average Transactions per year (the average amount of times clients buy from you per year)	2	2.2	
X	X	X	
Average profit per transaction (the average profit generated from a transaction)	$100	$110	
=	=	=	
Profit per year	$11,000	$16,093	46% increase

As you can see, a small 10% increase in each area results in a huge 46% increase in new clients... Exciting stuff!!

But imagine a 20% or 30% increase...

If you could double your results in each area that would mean a **1,600% increase in profits...**

I know it looks too easy... But it is if you do the work! Reaching and surpassing your desired income per hour can be easily attainable by concentrating on 4 areas in your business:

1. Increasing new **inquiries.**
2. Increasing the **conversion rate** of those inquiries to sales.
3. Increasing the **average transactions** per year of clients.
4. Increasing the **average profit** of each transaction.

Just a 1% increase per week will make a massive difference to your bottom line.

Eye-Opening Exercise –

In the Appendix, is a "Magic Profit Producing Formula" form and an example. Create your own, print it out, complete it with the results you have from the last 12 months of trading and file it in your "Business Growth File."

If you don't have 12 months of records then estimate the potential numbers, but be realistic!

90% of businesses I come across have no idea how many inquiries they get daily, weekly or monthly. Without measuring these you have no idea what is working and what is not.

You can't manage what you don't measure.

18 Ways To Generate Inquiries

Most Business Owners waste their money advertising. They listen to media salespeople who convince them to buy space or airtime and have great looking or sounding ads… But they just don't have the return on investment. 9 out of 10 times these great looking ads don't even get a single inquiry!

Now, I'm not saying that you should never listen to media salespeople. No, you should actually be very friendly with them because they can provide very important information on what's happening in the industry and in your local area. They visit many different businesses and know exactly what's working.

But they are trained to sell you space in their magazine or newspaper… or airtime on the radio or the TV. And they want you to keep buying the space or airtime on a regular basis. They don't know where your business is at, only you do and you have to make the decision of what medium to use and what message to send.

Media salespeople usually don't know the inner workings of direct response marketing and if they do treat them like gold. They rely on a design team consisting mostly of graphic artists. The design team will create a magnificent looking ad that will WOW you and in so doing they will have provided great service and probably over delivered.

Unfortunately, most businesses are struggling with cash flow, struggling with acquiring new clients and retaining the existing ones and great looking ads don't solve these problems.

Remember, Marketing is an investment, not an expense, so it is important that an ad gets the phone ringing or the client through the door. You should never have a budget for marketing.

If you run an ad that costs $200 and it brings in $1,000 worth of profit, are you going to run it continuously or are you going to be limited by a budget… it's a no-brainer! You run that ad continuously and don't change it. Even if you are bored of the ad your clients will tell you when they are bored of it when the returns drop off consistently over a few months.

It is important to test and measure constantly so that ads can be improved and the return on investment calculated and constantly improved.

So many businesses put ads out there and hope business is generated from them. I ask businesses if their ads work and they say "I think so, but it's getting our name out there."

Businesses cannot afford to have ads that are "getting them known" or "getting their name out there."

Advertising has to at least break-even initially; $1 spent on advertising should produce at least $1 of profit.

Then you should be aiming for a minimum return of investment of spending $1 on advertising to return $5 of profits and then improving on that again.

Test and measure task –

In the Appendix, is an "Advertising Return On Investment" form and an example.

These forms should be completed for every new ad or campaign.

Create your own, print it out, complete it and file them in your "Business Growth File."

Learning to write ads is beyond the content of this book but I'll provide a few basic pointers on writing great ads:

- Ads should never look like ads. People skim ads but read stories that are interesting.
- The headline is the most important part and should be benefit focused.
- Don't blatantly sell. Offer information that is useful with an invitation to call or come in for more.
- An offer should be so inviting that they would be crazy to ignore it.

If you would like more detailed information on writing great direct response ads visit
www.profitmarketing101.com

Now here's how to generate those inquiries:

Newspaper advertising

Newspapers are a common way to advertise your product or service. The rates are usually good and the return on investment can be good if used properly.

Think of your own habits when reading the newspaper. Generally, the headlines and pictures encourage people to read on. So your ad needs to have a great headline but also an amazing offer that will have them cutting the ad out and keeping it so they can contact you tomorrow.

Results should be seen within the first 3 days of the newspaper release. Don't be afraid to negotiate the ad insertion price and ask for the ad to be placed on the right page and within the first 5 pages of the newspaper. Often free editorials are available or an advertorial where an editorial is combined with an advertisement.

When something different or interesting happens in your business call the newspaper as they are always looking for stories and any publicity is good.

Press Releases

Fax or email your story to the local media outlets and encourage them to publish it. The story has to be newsworthy and worth publishing. Journalists have to fill the space in the newspaper so if you have a story that is well written and interesting they will consider publishing it.

It is a good idea to call before sending the article and to follow up afterward.

School Newsletter advertising

This is great cost-effective advertising. It shows credibility and trust by the school and is very effective at targeting parents and teachers.

Directories

Think of how you would try and locate the details of your business and make sure you are listed in each one of those. Some examples are:

- Telephone directory
- Yellow Pages
- Trade directories
- Online directories

You should make it incredibly easy for people to find your telephone number and address. If people can't find your details they will go to a competitor.

Recommended by a Friend

For a fraction of the effort and virtually no expense, a formalized referral system is very powerful. Most of your present clients were probably referred directly or indirectly. There is no better credibility than being referred by someone they trust. A referred client is usually pre-qualified and can be more profitable.

To get referrals all you need to do is ask. Make it part of your sales process. Tell your client how much you enjoyed dealing with them and are keen to attract more clients of their caliber. If you have provided the right service they will have no problem in referring their friends and colleagues. Volunteer to advise, talk to or meet with any of their friends without the expectation of a sale.

Radio advertising

Radio can be expensive but can have a great return on investment if your product or service has some urgency. People don't actively listen to the radio; it is usually on in the background so your ad must be very noticeable.

A local radio station where I live uses their own medium very effectively. They have a radio ad that comes on between 8 and 9 every weekday morning in which they advertise for people to come to a different daily location, and for 15 minutes they give away free product from a few businesses.

My wife loves this ad and listens for it every day. She has received free fake suntans, bakery products, gift vouchers and more. Not only do the businesses that take part get you to sample their product but they exchange this for your permission to accept any marketing material. People love free stuff and when they receive great service while taking up the free offer they may consider coming again. They will also tell their friends.

Magazine advertising

This advertising is great for reaching a targeted group of people. If your offer suits that particular target market the return on investment should be great, provided the offer is powerful enough.

Direct Mail

Direct mail is very cost-effective as it goes into the hands of a targeted audience. Direct mail pieces need to be written well to be effective. A formula that I use to write direct mail pieces is a benefit filled headline, then talk about the problem, aggravate the problem, talk about a solution, then the offer.

An even better impact can be had if the envelope is made lumpy as the letter then tends to go to the top of the pile. Lumpy letters can be achieved with the insertion of gimmicky items that relate to the content of the letter.

Some of the items I've received have been toy cars, teabags, a small packet of candy, coins, and pens. I love lumpy mail; it is always the first envelope I open because I love the excitement to see what's in there… I've known of very successful direct mail campaigns that were delivered in plastic water bottles and labeled.

Direct mail is very easy to learn. File any letters that made you want to buy, and borrow ideas.

Internet

Today it is imperative that every business has a website, even if it is a simple one-page website. More and more people search online for information and you have to have some presence online.

It has become incredibly cost-effective and simple to set up a simple website. You could have your sales catalog online with a simple email type order. Anybody looking for information could easily email you at 2.00am and you could respond the next morning.

The internet is a great source of income 24/7 and broadens the geographical area you can sell to. Not only could you be taking orders for your product or service but you could start selling information products related to your industry.

Vehicle Signage

Every one of your vehicles is potentially a mobile billboard that incurs a cost initially to be sign written but provides a return for the life of the vehicle. With the new vinyl signage, it is fairly easy to remove the signage before selling the vehicle.

Remember when the vehicle is moving it is very hard for people to read too much detail, so keep it simple. Be bold and different.

Shopping Centre Promotions

This is a very effective means of gathering potential client details in exchange for entry into a competition. I also find this strategy very effective in uncovering any product or service objections as people are keen to discuss these in the informal environment.

Business Cards

Most people underuse their business cards by only having their contact information on them. There is usually so much wasted space on them especially the back. Use them as a mini sales letter and have a great benefit-driven headline with some copy. This will explain in detail what your business is about and people will read it.

Stickers

Every product you send out should have a sticker attached to remind people where they purchased from. When I owned a telephone system installation business all the handsets had a small sticker attached under the handset.

If a user had a problem the number to call us was conveniently placed so they didn't have to search for it.

Network, Network, and Network

People will buy from credible people and networking is an easy way to build credibility quickly and hand out those mini sales letter type business cards. They are guaranteed to spark up some conversation.

Competitions

Competitions are the best tool for gathering a database of names and details quickly. People love the chance to win something for nothing. Most Business Owners wimp out here and offer prizes that are not great motivators to bring people in or get them to call.

If you want a few names, offer a small prize. But, to get a substantial list you need to offer a few prizes of substantial value.

I knew of a lady (Jane) with a small store offering various little gifts (average transaction profit was $21). Jane offered a trip for 2 to Hawaii which was valued at over $5,000. The local travel agent had done a deal and Jane paid less than $3,000.

Jane knew her clients average lifetime value was $945 so she required 3.2 clients to break even. The result was outstanding - 146 new clients over 30 days and 64% of her existing clients came and bought just to qualify.

To qualify for entry the clients had to spend $50 or more. This meant her average transaction profit jumped from $21 to $34.

Let's analyze this - Jane spent $3,000 for airline tickets to Hawaii and then spent $1,000 advertising this offer in the newspapers. Total cost $4,000. Her client's perception was to spend $50 for a chance to win this prize worth $5,000.

The results – existing clients generated a profit of $6,138, new clients generated a profit of $4,526. Total profit - $10,664 over and above normal trade.

The best part - 146 new clients, with a total average lifetime value of $137,970 that gave her permission to market to them regularly. Jane now runs a competition every 6 months!!

VIP Client Days

Have a special day for VIP clients and they can bring a friend. Offer the friend a gift for completing a survey form. Do these days when you receive new stock so VIP clients get to buy first. Your clients will love you for this.

Strategic Alliances

Another very powerful technique that results in having a sales force (that costs nothing) constantly recommending you. Think about other businesses that are not competitors but could compliment your service. Like the hairdresser and the beauty salon, the gardener with a window cleaner, the computer technician with a phone technician and create a one-stop shop by promoting each other.

I have found that this works better when a commission is involved; a small referral fee like 10% for a completed sale, as most often the relationship can be one-sided. But don't stop at recruiting one strategic alliance; find 10, 20 or 30. I certainly didn't mind paying the 10% in my businesses because it was much cheaper than having to advertise for that client. Any referral from a strategic alliance usually converts at 50% or better because there is so much credibility and the client is already pre-qualified.

This is an extremely powerful strategy and should be given a lot of your time. These strategic alliance relationships last a long time and create a powerful group of businesses that protect their clients. The businesses tend to lift their professionalism because if they let their other strategic alliances down they will be replaced by another business offering the same product or service.

In the past, some of my competitors become strategic alliances because they were better equipped to do certain jobs than I was so it was easier to refer the client.

Test and Measure -

Above you have fantastic ways for generating inquiries for your business. Some will work better than others but by testing and measuring you will determine which has a better return on investment than others. That allows you to focus on the ones producing the results but always have variety in your business.

15 Ways To Increase Your Conversion From Inquiry To Sale

I'm always amazed at the massive wastage that I witness on a daily basis.

I receive these beautiful glossy brochures in the mail that are costing the Business Owners a few dollars each at least… I browse through them and then they go in the round file commonly known as the bin.

Next week I get another one from the same company and again next week. There is no call to action, no effort to find out what I'm really looking for, no effort to get me into their business… just a massive waste!

I have on a few occasions actually gone into the business to view the product they are offering or to request a free quote for a service. In every case, in the last 12 months at least, I have never been followed up. I get a distinct feeling that the overall attitude is "Oh well if he wants the product or service, he'll come back."

Now I bet if I had to ask one of these Business Owners what their conversion rate is they would probably say 40% to 50%.

Most Business Owners guess because they don't really know, they have never measured their conversion. When I've advised businesses to measure their conversion rate for a week they are normally astounded with the results – the rate they thought was 40% is usually less than 15%.

The wonderful opportunity with a low conversion rate is it has a large potential for improvement. It is easier to double 15% than to double 40%.

Now if you've gone to the massive effort of getting people to call your business or walk through the door, don't waste the effort by letting them walk away. Most sales are made after the 5th contact with your business so at least get their contact details in exchange for a gift of some sort - free report or something with a high perceived value.

You must make the most out of every opportunity. Aim for 100% of the inquiries to turn into sales no matter how small the sale is… because it's the lifetime value of the client you are focused on.

Here's how to make it happen:

Collect all Potential Clients Details

Every business should have a monthly newsletter that is not only made up of offers but has some really useful information that is of value to the person reading it.

The information doesn't have to be related to the product or service offered.

I've seen great 1 page newsletters coming from shoe retailers with clean humorous stories that don't relate at all. But because of the humor, they had great readership, and people would ring up not wanting to buy shoes but to be included on the mailing list.

The collection of people's details and their permission to accept your marketing material is incredibly valuable in inviting people to VIP Client days, Exclusive new Stock Viewing Days and other similar events. Clients love feeling special.

Your database is a goldmine, but use it carefully. Respect it and keep it updated.

Give Away to Get Back

The law of reciprocation is very powerful. Do you remember a time when someone gave you something and you felt like you should reciprocate?

Always remember the lifetime value of your client... The quicker you get them in the system the better. So to achieve this, give away something for free!

You will be creating massive pain for your client
By them not doing business with you!

This is best explained with an example. Let's say a carpet cleaning service approaches you with the following offer:

We would like to come to your home and clean one bedroom for you. Our service is free and comes without any cost or obligation. All that we ask is that after we have cleaned your carpet free of charge, and you are completely delighted, that you will consider passing our name along to your friends and neighbors.

How can you say no to this?

It is what is called "The Irresistible Offer." Of course, everyone has a carpet that they would like cleaned and no one can get a better price than free! The condition is to simply pass the companies name along to their friends and neighbors but only if they are completely delighted with your work.

Easy...

You can imagine how the rest of the story goes. Once they see the clean carpet in their bedroom, the rest of the carpets look worse than ever, so they get you to clean the others.

Will some people take advantage of your free service?

YES! Of course, a small percentage will. But, the overwhelming majority will continue to do business with you and will gladly refer you to others.

Don't be afraid to give your service away. It is usually the cheapest form of client acquisition available. The return on investment is usually massive because clients love getting something for nothing and then experience the great service.

Remember the lifetime value of the client, how many times will they use your service? How many other clients will they refer? Will you get them on an annual type of contract where you do four carpet cleanings a year and maybe two emergency stain removals as needed?

You have now allowed them to sample your service and/or product for free, taken all the risk on yourself, made your offer irresistible, established trust and goodwill and set them up on a program to fill all of their needs in such a way as they never again have to worry about their carpets.

Remove all the Objections

Frequently asked question and answer forms and a strong risk reversal guarantee are very powerful ways to remove all buyer objections. In your business you will know of all the objections that you have come across, some seem trivial but a trivial objection will stop a client parting with their hard earned cash. Often clients won't tell you of their objections and you'll be wondering "why didn't they buy?"

In your inquiry process, there should always be documentation provided to the client that addresses all objections. In the appendix, I have included a sample of an FAQ form and a risk reversal guarantee. A great way to uncover any new objections is in a survey form provided to purchasers. People will tell you things in an anonymous survey form that they wouldn't tell you face to face. Also, some people forget, so the survey form will prompt them.

I've seen many guarantees from different business and they are usually not worth even having them. A good guarantee has to be powerful and it should reverse the risk so the client has absolutely nothing to worry about. Most Business Owners I talk to are frightened to offer a strong risk reversal type of guarantee because they are scared that people will abuse the guarantee and they will end up losing money.

The truth is there will always be someone that will take advantage of the guarantee and abuse the right but 99% of your clients will not take up the guarantee if your product is 80% as good as you say it is. The extra profits will be well worth the strong guarantee.

Look at your competitors, how many are offering a strong risk reversal guarantee? Put one in place and this immediately makes your business much more attractive to potential clients.

Be Different, Be Unique

If you are not different or unique the only other way to attract clients is on price… And that leads to certain business death.

You need to work out what is unique about your business. Why should people buy from you? Define your unique selling proposition. Why is your product or service better than your competitor? Make it meaningful, something that the clients will place a high value on.

Unique businesses have no competition because no-one else sells the same package or provides it the same way. Once you have defined this uniqueness shout it out to the world. Let everyone know.

If you don't think your business is unique then make it unique. Add extra value to your service; add things, change things, charge differently. Simple examples are having a rewards program, buy 10 get the 11th free. It costs your business next to nothing but makes your business different which attracts attention.

Collect Testimonials and Display Them Proudly

Credibility is imperative and the best credibility is when other clients say how wonderful your product or service is. Collecting testimonials should be part of your after sales process. But make sure they are great testimonials by asking for the right information in testimonials provided.

A testimonial that reads
"I implemented what Ian said and increased my sales"
is not going to be nearly as effective as
"I increased my profits from an average $2,006 per month to $4,980 per month by implementing only 3 strategies Ian suggests. I can't wait to implement the next 3."

It is also important to have a full name and a business name provided with the testimonial to add to the credibility. It's a 2-way street you get the testimonial and they get the exposure.

Testimonials should be supplied with every bit of sales documentation that leaves the business. A great idea is to frame them and display them proudly on a wall in your office next to your awards and certificates. People love reading them.

Demonstrate Your Product or Service

People tend to buy with their eyes. I'm guilty of this, I'll go to a trade show and see a tool that does something easier and quicker and will buy it after seeing the demonstration. I didn't need the tool before the demonstration but when I saw the demonstration it reminded me of times in the past when I could have used that tool.

If you can't show your product or service create a video or DVD that people can watch and see a demonstration. These can be cheaply produced and very cost-effective with a great WOW factor.

Make Sure All Payments Can Be Accepted Easily

I can't tell you how many times a business has lost my business because they wouldn't accept my credit card. I cannot believe in this modern day and age there are still businesses out there that won't accept credit cards because of the extra charges. How much business are they losing by not accepting the setup costs and the extra bank charges?

People expect different payment methods so you need to cater for that. Make it easy to do business with you.

Have Payment Plans

Some clients would love to buy your product or service but need to save for it as they just don't have the cash now. Always have a payment plan setup either financed by your business or through a 3rd party business to allow clients to pay over a period of time.

When I owned my telephone system installation business I made more profit if a client bought on a 24-month plan rather than paid cash. Our cash flow was great as we had recurring income and invariably at the end of the contract the client would upgrade to a new system and sign up for another 24 months. It provides loyalty because the condition of the contract was that any repairs, maintenance or changes to the installation had to be completed by us. It was a win/ win situation for both parties.

Never Provide Quotes

That got your attention, didn't it! You've probably been providing free quotes ever since you started in business. What is a quote? Basically, it says that you get xyz product or service for $xyz.

If you continue to provide quotes you are leaving the door wide open for people to compare your product and service on price only. You will lose far more often than win.

So if I'm saying don't provide quotes what do you use… A well-constructed sales letter that is designed to convert 100% of the time. And if it doesn't convert, it is because the client decided not to continue with the purchase of the product or service.

Now you may have a quote pad or book or a similar way of providing a quote very quickly, but this system comes with a high failure rate. Would it not be better to spend more time creating a letter that creates a lasting impression and provides a reason for you to follow up and converts at 80% to 100% of the time?

See the Sales Letter example in the Appendix.

Why would Sales letters convert so much better than quotes?

Because:
1. They will be different to everyone else's which shows you've taken the effort and the time, which clients appreciate.
2. The conversational style creates a relationship which provides an opportunity to follow up on.
3. You can offer to discuss the deal further if maybe there are budget constraints etc.
4. Sales letters are designed to get the price out of the way quickly and focus on the benefits later leaving a lasting impression.

5. Feelings can be incorporated into the letter.
6. Testimonial forms and FAQ forms can be added.
7. A risk reversal guarantee, value-added offers and a call to action can be included.

Quotes are saying -
"I don't have the time for you because you are not buying today, here's the price, take it or leave it."

While sales letters are saying –
"I've got time for you, I'm prepared to go the extra mile, I want to create a relationship with you for life and make sure you get the best all-round deal."

Your focus must always be on the lifetime value of the client. It may seem like extra work for small returns initially but once you have that client in your system you can work on extracting the full lifetime value of them.

I have had huge success whenever I have implemented this strategy in businesses. It's almost as if clients feel bad buying elsewhere because you have gone to so much effort. The feedback from clients was that they were impressed with how much we cared… it was a huge winner.

Follow Up

Most businesses I come across are frightened to follow up. It's crazy… they are worried about people getting angry about them following up. People are busy and businesses that follow up multiply their conversion rates hugely.

The client has made the effort to enquire, has trusted you enough to accept a sales letter or leave their details. They have said "yes, I am interested" but then life has taken over.

Don't leave it too long to follow up and always remember to be genuinely interested in their life, always look to enhance the relationship – it doesn't always have to be a hard sell.

Remember a "no" today could turn into a "yes" next week or next year. Clients could have a change in their financial status because of a pay rise or similar. Never get disheartened.

If they don't buy, ask for feedback or referrals.

Cross-Sell or Down-Sell

Remember we are talking about converting the client from enquiring to buying. So if they walk in wanting a specific product or service and it is clearly out of their budget, offer them some other alternative or even a payment plan.

Make Sure You And Your Staff Know Your Product or Service Inside Out

I get incredibly frustrated when I intend to buy something, have my credit card in my hand ready to pay… but just need some more information… and the staff member can't answer my questions!! aaaaarghh

It frustrates me so much that I don't care if the product is more expensive somewhere else. As long as my questions can be answered, my objections put to rest and I feel confident buying – that's where I'll spend my money.

Some businesses hire people to answer the phone or greet people as they walk in with the intention of training them about the product or service as they go… this mistake will cost you massively in lost sales. Don't do it!

Your business is only as good as your worst employee! Hopefully, your worst employee is not you?

Ask For That Sale

A common mistake for Business Owners is to build the relationship, do all the hard work supplying sales letters and following up and forgetting to ask for the sale. They assume that the sale will just naturally happen.

Buyers need to be held by the hand sometimes. If you have got to the stage of answering all the objections then you are allowed to think that it is a done deal and ask for the sale.

Ask For Feedback

Your clients have the answers to every problem in your business that you may or may not know about. Very often Business Owners have the blinkers on, not intentionally, and don't see things from a client's perspective.

Feedback from clients and potential clients is very powerful in finding out what you are doing right, what you are doing wrong and how they think you could improve. People need an incentive to give you the information, so usually a smaller competition will do the trick well.

Ask them!!

Measure Conversion Rates

You can only manage what you can measure. Test and measure your conversion with a simple spreadsheet. List all inquiries in one column with another column to mark yes or no as they convert or not. This tool will also help to keep track of the follow-up, as you need a yes or no to complete the conversion column.

If your conversion is low, go back and look at what is being said to the client verbally and on paper. A simple sentence change or a change in what is being said to clients can easily double your conversion.

7 Ways To Increase The Number Of Transactions

You've now learned how to get the inquiries flowing in and ensure they are converting well so the next step is convincing your clients to buy more often.

It's amazing how many people will say and do whatever it takes to get a one-time sale rather than taking the time to understand the client's actual needs. Sometimes what the client actually needs is much less than originally thought. Being honest with them makes them remember you for a long time.

I found some unscrupulous real estate agents in my short time in the game. The agents were paid on commission and buyers were deliberately steered towards properties with higher values or potential issues would not be disclosed because they didn't want to discourage the buyer.

In most cases these little non-disclosures came back and haunted them later on.

Now, by now, you should fully understand that each person has a lifetime buying value. So it is important that you collect their details, build a strong relationship, look after them well, give them special treatment, tell them you appreciate them, keep in constant contact with them and keep them coming back.

Here's how:

VIP Client Days

Clients need special service and treating them like they are special will have a big impact. I know of a lady that owns a women's shoe store. Every time new stock would arrive she would open her shop after hours for a few hours, invite her best clients, serve nibblies and refreshments while they looked over the new stock.

Not only did this result in quick sales because the clients wanted to be the first to have the new range but it further reinforced the Business Owner and Client relationship.

Tell Clients What Else You Offer

I can't tell you of the number of times I've heard people say *"I didn't know xyz business sold those."* Never assume that people will know or remember what you sell… you have to remind them over and over again. One way is with a newsletter which can be delivered by mail or via email.

Don't ever think you are reminding them too many times because you have to be at the front of their mind when they are ready to buy.

Keep In Regular Contact

Regular contact with your clients is absolutely imperative. This could be done with a newsletter, email, postcard, lumpy mail, invitation or phone call. But keep the excitement, don't get boring or your material will end up in the bin.

Think of ways to make clients want to open your mail, make it memorable. Clients love stories so run a monthly story on an employee, a supplier, a client or a strategic alliance. Provide some history and include some humor.

Client contact should happen, at the minimum, once a month but I have seen better results when the client contact was reduced to every 2nd week.

Your business is not a priority for clients so they will forget you if you don't remind them.

Diversify

If the product or service clients buy from you is usually a one-off then you need to find ways to encourage repeat sales. Examples are if you sell 2nd hand cars you could offer servicing of the car, car detailing, tires and car accessories.

A carpet cleaner could have a 3 monthly carpet maintenance and deodorizing treatment or maybe a strategic alliance that offers a window clean every 3 months and the carpet cleaner receives a commission or referral fee.

Offer Product Upgrades

The fashion industry is a great example of this. Every new season we are encouraged to throw out the old clothes and replace them with new to keep up with the latest fashion.

The electronics industry continues to provide new models that operate better, do a better job, and are easier to use… always new and improved.

How could you apply this to your business?

Offer Maintenance Contracts

If you can offer a maintenance contract on the product or service you sell, you will know exactly when that item needs replacing. Maintenance contracts usually result in upgrades or the purchase of accessories along the way.

Remind the Client

Dentists, Florists, Mechanics remind their clients all the time with a note in the mail or a phone call, *"By the way, it's been 6 months since your last check up,"* or *"its Valentines Day next month."*

I've found in the past that it works better by sending out a note and then following up with a call. The call is when the best conversion is likely to happen.

12 Ways To Increase The Transaction Size

You've got the inquiries flowing in, you're converting them really well, and the clients are coming in more often. Now you need to get them to spend more money when they do spend.

It's the old *"Would you like fries with that?"* story. One little sentence adds millions to the bottom line. So easy, so simple!

How can you apply that to your business? Remember these clients are already committed to buying from you, they are in buying mode.

Here are some ideas:

Extended Warranty

I bought my son a video game for his birthday for $39.95 and they cleverly offered me a lifetime warranty for the game for $3. Now the only problem I've heard anyone having with a game is that it won't work straight out of the box which a return to the shop will very quickly get fixed without lifetime warranty.

Other than that they tend to work forever, but for $3 and the way it was worded I had no problem paying the extra $3. Now if 50% of the games are sold with the $3 lifetime warranty I think they will have been very successful with increasing their transaction size.

I guarantee if in 2 years time the game has a problem we won't even remember the lifetime warranty – in fact, the game will be well and truly obsolete by then.

Don't make the mistake of thinking the extra $3 is not worth the effort. $3 times by 100 transactions every week will increase your profit by $15,600 per year.

Increase Your Prices

Just do it, add 10% to all your prices today. A small percentage of clients will notice and object but the extra profit from the other clients that don't even notice will more than cover this.

Sell by adding value and selling the benefits. Earlier we spoke about making your business unique so by doing this there is no other product or service to compare it to.

You have very little to lose and a massive amount to gain… so increase your prices by 10% today.

Cross-Sell and Up-Sell

There are always other add-on products or services you can sell your clients like buying a suit and being offered a shirt or a tie.

If you have only one product or service to sell you need to find other products or services to offer as cross-sells or up-sells. It may mean creating a deluxe version of your product or service or using a strategic alliance as a cross-sell. Like the gardener offering the services of the window cleaner.

Often in the sale process it is easy to get caught up in the sale and to forget to cross-sell. I suggest you make checklists so employees remember to offer the cross-sells – like the paint shop having a checklist reminding the client they will need a roller, a brush, brush cleaners, etc.

Package Deals

Like the paint shop offering the client a roller, a paint brush and cleaners… and risking the client only taking a brush, how about having a package deal where everything is included for a discount of $X. Now the client starts thinking that they don't really need all the extra bits but the package deal is so good they'll take it.

This is a great strategy to move the stock that doesn't sell well. The packages could also be decorated to become gifts.

Payment Terms

Having payment terms for bundled items works well if the client has a budget but would like the bundle. Make it easy for them to upgrade without having to pay for it right now. It is often better to have a good client take your stock knowing it will be paid for in a month or two rather than having it sitting on your shelf gathering dust.

Cater for Impulse Buyers

Supermarkets do this really well by having chocolates and magazines at checkout points. Clients waiting to be served are reminded the chocolates and magazines are there. They are strategically placed so that clients give in and buy them. Have a look at your checkout points, what could you be adding for those impulse buyers?

Spend $50 or More And Get XYZ

Remember the story I told you earlier about Jane offering a free entry into a competition to win a trip for 2 to Hawaii. The condition was they had to spend $50 or more. This strategy immediately boosted her average transaction size because people wanted to qualify. They would sometimes buy anything just to make up the $50 spend.

How could you do this in your business?

Accept any Type of Payment

I've spoken about this before but it is incredibly important in increasing your average transaction size. If you only accept cash, or you only accept Mastercard and VISA and don't accept AMEX then you will turn away a lot of business.

I love the rewards I receive when using my AMEX card so if 2 competitors are offering a similar product but the one accepts AMEX, guess where I'm buying?

Focus on A-Grade Clients

A-grade clients are the ones that don't complain, pay full price, tell you how wonderful you are, give you great feedback and then tell all their friends how great you are.

Identify those clients and nurture them like your own child. Provide them with exceptional service and make sure they are the first to know about any new stock, any new deals, any new staff, when you are going on holidays, etc… They will love it and purchase more often.

Offer Total Convenience

Offer to deliver to their home, offer to pack and send anywhere in the world, offer to gift wrap, offer to take orders over the phone, offer to provide service after hours... whatever it takes to provide convenience for the client provide it.

Remember the lifetime value of the client!!

There is a small little shop downtown that sells Biltong (dried meat.) Having grown up in Zimbabwe we just about grew up on the stuff. Now in Australia it's not freely available and if it is available it tastes like cardboard, except from this little shop. The trouble is I live 20 minutes from this shop and because I can live without it I'll only buy Biltong when I happen to be driving past the shop. The shop also sells other goodies that I'll buy when I go in but again I could live without them. So I probably spend $40 every 3rd month on average.

Now if the owner offered to deliver this $40 package to my house every month I would gladly accept because of the convenience... heck I would even pay a few dollars for delivery. She would then go from selling me $160 worth of product per year to $480. An increase of $$320 or 200% for one client... what about if 20 clients accepted this service or 40!!

Very simple but unfortunately people get busy in their businesses doing and don't do things smarter.

Never Ever Discount

Never ever discount, because discounting is a disease that eats away profits and will end in certain business death.

You can add value by offering other product with a high perceived value – like a special report that costs you nothing but has a $50 value to the client. Your client thinks you are giving away $50 of product but you are actually giving away nothing. Or you could offer free delivery… anything that has a very low dollar value to you.

It's not what you give away, but how valuable people perceive it to be.

If you discount people will hear about it and more people will ask for discounts. I know because our local Electrical Wholesaler offered me a discount even though I didn't ask for one. So now every time I go in there I ask for a discount because it is expected.

Know Your Numbers

Every business should know exactly what its profit margins are on each product and by looking at the sales every month you can calculate which are your popular products and services. A product with a high-profit margin may be the slowest moving product.

If you know your numbers you will know exactly where the best potential for profit is. Pick the low hanging fruit first – go after the easiest sales first but always focus on improving in every area.

Know Your Costs, Know Your Profit

Well now you know how to get the inquiries, you know how to convert those inquiries to a sale, you know how to improve the amount of times clients buy and how to increase the amount clients spend each time.

Fantastic information but if every time you sell an item or product you make a loss, then what I've just told you will send you plummeting to the ground faster than not knowing this stuff.

I can give you many examples of where Business Owners have taken the cost of the product added a profit margin and sold at that price. They've then noticed a competitor selling at a lower price and have trimmed their margin to match the price.

This is a recipe for disaster. Compete on price and you will attract clients that are price focused only and these are usually D-grade clients. D-grade clients want the cheapest possible price and then delay paying as much as possible while complaining about the service. You don't want these clients. D-grade clients are the ones you refer to your competitors.

In the appendix, I have included a basic profit and loss schedule with an example. If you are using a point of sale system or an accounting package then you probably already have this information. However, most Business Owners look at their profit and loss statement once a year and are usually surprised at the results.

Your Accountant is the best person for accounting advice. I am not an Accountant nor do I play one on TV. I am just pointing out why you need to be looking at your profit and loss statement more frequently.

Every week you should be closely analyzing your profit and loss statement with one goal in mind - to increase the bottom line. The bottom line is the profit left over after paying all your expenses and overheads.

At this stage you have overheads and expenses. When you buy product to sell, you add a margin which is your profit. That margin has to pay for your overheads like the rent, electricity, telephone etc. After paying the overheads, what is left over is the bottom line which you are able to pay yourself from.

Some overheads are fixed, like the rent you pay for your premises but some are variable like the telephone. If you do more business the telephone usage will increase.

The overheads you have in place will allow you to do a certain amount of business. If you exceed that amount of business you may need to look for bigger premises to accommodate the extra business hence increasing your overheads.

So the trick is to maximize the bottom line within the overhead structure you have now. If there is massive growth in your business you will be forced to increase the overheads with more staff or a bigger office. But if you go to that stage you need to maximize the profit at that level again.

In most cases people grow their business quickly and increase their bottom line substantially only to have it eroded when they started hiring full-time staff or upgraded to bigger premises. Your profit and loss schedule will highlight this problem before you implement it. For example by inserting the potential costs associated with an extra staff member the bottom line change will indicate how much extra income will be required to pay for this.

It is natural for Business Owners to look at profit and loss schedules, be dissatisfied with the bottom line and then look where they can cut costs.

Cutting costs can save 10% here and there but you are far better focusing your energy on growing the income. Certainly, make sure your costs are not excessive but 90%

of your focus should be on multiplying the income using the strategies discussed in this book. Cost cutting is a very short-term solution that will probably end up making you busier and more stressed. Income growth is the long-term solution.

Now Take Massive Action

The income increasing strategies you have now learned have worked for thousands of businesses. I have used them in my own businesses and I have seen others use them very effectively in many different businesses, in many different industries.

But I've seen it too often... Most clients don't implement anything because they say *"they are too busy!"* They don't understand that this will help them get their life back and a bonus will be a substantially improved income.

Other clients will try one strategy, increase their profits by 100% or more and stop there. It's almost like they've achieved their desired hourly income per hour and they don't need anymore. It's crazy!

Why would you stop if one strategy has worked so well? Keep going, keep implementing, and keep growing that income, keep multiplying that profit...

Some strategies can be applied at no cost while others need an investment but in conjunction, they will produce dramatic results.

So, you have the tools, you have the Magic Formula, you know what to be looking for so there is absolutely no excuse not to double, triple or quadruple your income in the next 12 months… RIGHT!!

All it will take is implementation…

To help here is a step by step Action Plan:

Step 1 Test and Measure

These measurement processes need to be put into place so you can manage what you are measuring:

- **Measure and record all inquiries** – ask every potential client how they found out about your business. This will tell you what advertising is working.
- **Measure the conversions** – from every inquiry and record the ones that buy. Remember some clients don't buy straight away so keep accurate records.
- **Measure the number of transactions** - how many times are clients coming in and buying again.
- **Transaction value** – Take the total week's dollar sales figure and divide it by the amount of transactions.
- **Profit and loss** – update weekly and compare to past results.

It will take a few weeks before you see some sort of trend happening. When you have 12 months of past information it becomes easier because you can improve on last years result. Comparing one month to the same month last year means all factors are equal - the season, other events at that time of year and anything else that could affect sales.

Step 2 Grow The Business

Now you've got your starting point. You know exactly what the numbers are in your business. Now let's grow them continuously.

Go back through each idea I've given you and choose 3 from each of the 4 categories in the Magic Profit Producing Formula.

Use the form on the next page and write them down:

I'm going to boost Inquiries by:

1)
2)
3)

I'm going to boost my conversion by:

1)
2)
3)

I'm going to boost the number of transactions by:

1)
2)
3)

I'm going to boost the transaction size by:

1)
2)
3)

Now implement what you have written down.

Remember **PERSISTENCE** is the name of the game. Some ads you will try and they won't work, but now you know to measure the return on investment of that ad – if it doesn't work move on. Persist until you get there.

Don't concentrate on only one area of the Magic Profit Producing Formula; you need to work on all 4. Start implementing one of the ideas in each area and then start on the 2nd and so on. This is a process that requires constant monitoring, testing, measuring and improving for the life of the business.

While some ideas work in the business now, as it matures others may work better. Just keep working on improving all areas of the Magic Profit Producing Formula.

This process is guaranteed to work provided you work it!

Start it NOW, start it today but just start…

Final Words

There is only so much I can put in this book before I completely overwhelm you with information. I have provided the most effective strategies.

But business is a game and often ideas can be taken from other successful industries and modified to suit your business.

Always be on the lookout. Adopt and adapt, watch how other businesses encourage new clients to buy and then retain those clients. Experience their service and analyze what they are doing. Keep and file their sales copy, make notes of the process they use, listen to what their staff are saying.

It's so much easier than you think. Just start being observant. Keep a notebook at all times and make notes when you notice a marketing technique that draws you in or an ad with a great headline. Anything that makes you want to buy.

Any great sales material can be adapted to your business when you need it. Direct mail that you receive in the mail is a great source of ideas and normally a great deal of thought has gone into the layout of the letter to ensure a great conversion. Don't throw them away but use them as a basis for your direct mail. Don't ever copy them word for word, but notice the headline, the formula they use, the language, the layout, the guarantee and learn from them.

If you don't believe a concept or strategy will be applicable in your business, don't reject the idea. Think of how a portion can be used or how it can be adapted.

By observing you will find new ways and new ideas continuously… your income growth can be limitless.

But don't be overcome by information overload as most do. The money comes when you apply what you have learned.

So go out there and succeed by applying what you have learned!

Enjoy Your Success… always remember…

"Life is a journey…
So enjoy the ride along the way!"

About The Author

Ian McConnell is an educator and author dedicated to helping Business Owners earn more in less time.

Ian has owned many businesses, most of which were started from nothing.

They range from one extreme - an Electrical Contracting business - to the other extreme - a model train how to website - with many brick and mortar and online businesses in between.

He is a successful business entrepreneur and has been able to apply the strategies in this book many times. Not only to create great cash flow but to grow the businesses into valuable assets that resulted in being very attractive to buyers.

Ian knows first hand the challenges Business Owners face.

He knows what it's like to have the skills to complete the job well and then be faced with the frustrations in having to constantly encourage new inquiries, convince clients to buy more often and then get them to spend more.

When he learned the formula he realized that business wasn't about being the best at the job, but having the basic principles of business in place that guaranteed success.

He learned that no matter what business he was in, he had to become a master of marketing that business. Once he perfected this he had the cash flow to put all the staff and systems in place.

**For more "real business" tips
visit www.ProfitMarketing101.com**

Appendix

The following forms are provided for your use:

- Earnings per hour form
- Daily time form
- Client lifetime value form
- Magic profit producing formula form
- Advertising return on investment form
- Profit and loss form

The following examples are provided for your use:

- Earnings per hour example
- Daily time form example
- Client lifetime value example
- Advertising return on investment example
- Profit and loss example
- FAQ example
- Risk reversal guarantee example
- Sales letter example

Earnings Per Hour Form

Desired earnings per hour $_____

date	Actual earnings / hr	Date	Actual earnings / hr	date	Actual earnings / hr

Earnings per Hour Form (EXAMPLE)

Desired earnings per hour $52.00

Date	Actual earnings / hr	date	Actual earnings/ hr	date	Actual earnings / hr
1/2/2020	A$22.86				
1/9/2020	A$22.96				
1/16/2020	A$21.42				
1/23/2020	$22.35				
1/30/2020	A$23.56				
2/6/2020	A$25.90				
2/13/2020	A$26.54				
2/20/2020	A$26.65				
2/27/2020	A$28.92				
3/5/2020	A$29.32				
3/12/2020	A$33.56				
3/19/2020	A$34.21				
3/26/2020	A$33.18				
3/30/2020	A$33.58				
4/2/2020	A$41.52				

Daily Time Form

Date - _____

	Task	Hours	Category
7.00			
7.30			
8.00			
8.30			
9.00			
9.30			
10.00			
10.30			
11.00			
11.30			
12.00			
12.30			
1.00			
1.30			
2.00			
2.30			
3.00			
3.30			
4.00			
4.30			
5.00			

Daily Time Form (EXAMPLE)

Date – Monday 4/26/2020

	Task	Hours	Category
7.00	Opened shop and vacuumed floor	0.5	Waste
7.30	Checked appointment book	0.5	Admin
8.00	Loaded van with material for jobs	0.5	Waste
8.30	Travel to University	0.5	Income
9.00	Started Uni job	2	Income
9.30			
10.00			
10.30			
11.00	Uni job finished travel to Smith job	0.5	Income
11.30	Arrived at Smith job and started	1.5	Income
12.00			
12.30			
1.00	Stopped for lunch	0.5	Waste
1.30	Continued Smith job	1.5	Income
2.00			
2.30			
3.00	Completed Smith job travel to shop	0.5	Income
3.30	Arrived at shop and offloaded van	0.5	Waste
4.00	Updated jobcards	0.5	Admin
4.30	Invoiced clients	0.5	Admin
5.00	Closed shop		
8.00	Started quote for Kennedy job	2	Admin
10.00	Completed quote		
	TOTAL	12	
	Waste 2hrs 17%, Admin 3.5hrs 29%		
	Income-producing 6.5hrs 54%		

Client Lifetime Value Form

Date - _____

Average profit generated on first purchase	A

Average profit generated after initial purchase	
Average profit per purchase after initial purchase	
MULTIPLY BY	x
Average amount of Purchases per year after initial purchase	
MULTIPLY BY	x
Average amount of years that they will remain as a client	
Average profit generated after initial purchase TOTAL	B

A + B = Average Client Lifetime Value	

Client Lifetime Value Form (EXAMPLE)

Date – Monday 5/12/2020

Average profit generated on first purchase	A$156.36

Average profit generated after initial purchase	
Average profit per purchase after initial purchase	A$22.58
MULTIPLY BY	x
Average amount of Purchases per year after initial purchase	12
MULTIPLY BY	x
Average amount of years that they will remain as a client	8
Average profit generated after initial purchase TOTAL	A$2,167.68

A + B = Average Client Lifetime Value	A$2,324.04

Magic Profit Producing Formula

Date range _____ to _____

	Previous Results	Todays Results	Change
Inquiries (the total number of potential clients that call or walk in to your business)			
X	X	X	
Conversion Rate (the percentage of potential clients that you convince to buy)			
=	=	=	
No. of Clients (they have bought)			
X	X	X	
Average Transactions per year (the average amount of times clients buy from you per year)			
X	X	X	
Average profit per transaction (the average profit generated from a transaction)			
=	=	=	
Profit per year			

Magic Profit Producing Formula (EXAMPLE)

Date range: 2/1/20 to 2/8/20

	Previous Results	Todays Results	Change
Inquiries (the total number of potential clients that call or walk in to your business)	2500	2588	3.5%
X	X	x	
Conversion Rate (the percentage of potential clients that you convince to buy)	22%	28%	27.3%
=	=	=	
No. of Clients (they have bought)	550	724	31.6%
X	X	X	
Average Transactions per year (the average amount of times clients buy from you per year)	2	2	0%
X	X	X	
Average profit per transaction (the average profit generated from a transaction)	A$100	A$112	12%
=	=	=	
Profit per year	A$110,000	A$162,176	47.4%

Advertising Return On Investment

Date – _____

Advertisement – _____

Product/ service offered – _____

Media - _____

Insertion date – _____

Cost to produce ad	
Cost to run ad	
Total ad cost	

Profit expected for each sale	
No of sales to breakeven	
No of inquiries from ad	
No of sales from ad	
Return on investment – (No of sales from ad x profit from each sale – total ad cost)	
Return on investment divided by total ad cost x 100	

Advertising Return On Investment (EXAMPLE)

Date – Wednesday 3/20/2020

Advertisement – Free Air conditioner maintenance

Product/ service offered – 1 hr of maintenance labor

Media - newspaper

Insertion date – 3/25/2020 to 4/15/2020

Cost to produce ad	A$112.00
Cost to run ad	A$565.00
Total ad cost	A$677.00

Profit expected for each sale	A$125.00
No of sales to breakeven	5.4
No of inquiries from ad	45
No of sales from ad	34
Return on investment – (No of sales from ad x profit from each sale – total ad cost)	A$3,573.00
Return on investment divided by total ad cost x 100	527%

Profit and Loss

	month	month	month	month	month	month	TOTAL
INCOME							
product							
product							
product							
product							
TOTAL							
EXPENSES							
expense							
expense							
expense							
expense							
expense							
expense							
expense							
expense							
expense							
expense							
expense							
TOTAL							
Income less expenses							

Profit and Loss (EXAMPLE)

	Jan 20	Feb 20	Mar 20	Apr 20	May 20	Jun 20	TOTAL
INCOME							
services	2,500		4,014			2,121	8,635
installs	1,020	1,521		1,987	2,564		7,092
cable	3,021		2,104			1,541	6,677
TOTAL	6,541	1,521	6,118	1,987	2,564	3,662	22,393

	Jan 20	Feb 20	Mar 20	Apr 20	May 20	Jun 20	TOTAL
EXPENSES							
Product cost	654	152	611	198	256	366	2,237
Rent	1,000	1,000	1,000	1,000	1,000	1,000	6,000
electricity	311	311	311	311	311	311	1,866
telephone	123	111	98	65	124	135	656
Car loan	405	405	405	405	405	405	2,430
petrol	65	67	74	105	56	62	429
insurance	112	112	112	112	112	112	672
stationery	32			65		47	144
postage	18	14	8	21	32	7	100
computor	45			23	8		76
TOTAL	2,765	2,172	2,619	2,305	2,304	2,445	14,610

Income less expenses	3,776	-651	3,499	-318	260	1,217	7,783

Frequently Asked Questions (EXAMPLE)

What type of payment do you accept?

We will accept any payment by any means. The usual payment method is with a credit card (we accept all) check or cash. Should you have any suggestions we would certainly listen to them.

I would like my air-conditioner serviced on a weekend, is that possible?

Yes, that is possible and we do not charge any extra for the service after our normal trading hours. Please go to our online booking service and enter the details and day required.

Your guarantee states that my new hairstyle will be liked by most of my friends. What happens if they don't like it?

Our aim is to make sure you are totally happy. If your friends say they don't like it just come back in and we will redo whatever you would like us to do at no charge. If you are still not happy we will pay our competitor to restyle your hair.

Do you offer discounts to Pensioners?

Yes, we certainly do. Pensioners receive a 30% discount every day of the week and a free basket of fruit.

Why is your service so expensive?

Our service is priced to provide a great level of customer service and a quality product. We recruit the best staff possible and pay them well. By doing this our clients are always assured of receiving the best possible service and the highest quality product.

Why do you only offer green?

Over the years we have tried many different colors and green is the only color that stands up to the high temperatures and extreme conditions. We would prefer to use blue or red as suggested by many of our clients but unfortunately blue and red just do not handle the conditions and have to be changed twice as often. By using green we are saving our clients on average $1,022 per year.

Risk Reversal Guarantees (EXAMPLE)

100% money back guarantee – No conditions apply

We guarantee that you will be ecstatic with our service and the repairs to your car. Should you not be 100% satisfied we will pay a competitor of your choice to complete the repairs for you.

100% iron clad guarantee

You have 6 full weeks to use your portable air conditioner. And if for any reason you are not absolutely 100% satisfied with your purchase – call us and we will collect the air conditioner and promptly and courteously refund you in full. No questions asked. It's that simple.

100% money back guarantee

You have 365 days to examine and use the home renovation course. If for any reason you want a full refund, just return the kit and you'll get your money back immediately. NO questions asked. No hassle. No "fine print." I want you thrilled with what you receive in my Kit or you request a full refund.

Sales Letter (EXAMPLE)

Good morning Mr. Smith

Thank you for taking the time to show me through your property on Monday. It certainly is an impressive location and your home allows you to take in the wonderful views across the Nooder Plains.

From what you told me you would prefer a more durable hardwood floor that is lighter in color. The floor is to be low maintenance and we are to provide an ongoing service to clean the surface.

We discussed an installation price of $15,544 for a plateplux floor, color agura. An ongoing charge of $144 per month is applicable with a number of services.

I'll explain…

You'll be receiving a professional and thorough monthly cleaning service using high tech hardwood flooring cleaning fluid. This new product is guaranteed by us to leave no residue and provide a non-slip surface.

The fluid highlights the natural tone of the hardwood and has properties that guard against termites. That means a much longer lasting hardwood floor. In addition to this service, we pay particular attention to the cleanliness in the hard to get at corners.

Mr. Smith, we offer a 100% money back guarantee, so all the risk is on us. The floor is guaranteed for 5 years but in addition to this if you are not totally satisfied with any part of the floor, we will repair it. Should you still not be satisfied after the repair we will pay a competitor of your choice to repair it for you.

Mr. Smith, my direct number is 123 456 789. Please don't hesitate to call should you have any further questions.

With best regards

Ian B McConnell

P.S. We are able to start this job on Friday and complete it within 7 days. I will call on Tuesday to confirm the details of this letter and perhaps confirm the start date.

Thank You

Thank you for taking the time to read this book. I am sincerely grateful. It has taken me decades to learn this stuff and I wrote this book so that you don't have to to go through the same school of hard knocks that I went through.

This book is a great start, but if you want more, I suggest you go to www.ProfitMarketing101.com and join us there.

You will also get access to all the downloadable forms and spreadsheets in this book.

I wish you well and the best of success in your business. Please send me your comments, questions and feedback via my website contact form at
www.ProfitMarketing101.com/contact

Thank you,
Ian McConnell

www.ingramcontent.com/pod-product-compliance
Lightning Source LLC
Chambersburg PA
CBHW071606220526
45469CB00003B/1129